January and Mondays are the same

Emma Heath

BookLeaf Publishing

India | USA | UK

Presentation by *BookLeaf Publishing*

Web: www.bookleafpub.com

E-mail: info@bookleafpub.com

ISBN: 9789360940317

First edition 2024

*Dedicated to every single mother who
thought at one time that they were failing
but still got to the end.*

ACKNOWLEDGEMENT

Thankyou to my children for teaching me about the joys of life. Thankyou to present and past lovers for teaching me about love in all forms. Thankyou to romantic fiction for teaching me to dream.

PREFACE

"Why worry? If you've done the very best you can, then worrying won't make it any better"- Walt Disney

A quote to absolutely live by.

The hope of this collection of poems is to inspire strength within the reader that they may have lost along their way at some point. To inspire prioritising integrity and kindness in a world filled with the opposites. To believe in love, trust and forgiveness but at most to believe in themselves.

January 1st

You start the year
Fragile and unclear
Hazy thoughts running wild
Just like a little child
Getting lost in the wood
Of what could

You crawl into bed
With a throbbing head
"I'll start tomorrow"
Said again with such sorrow
And drift off into dreams
Of your screams

Never alone

For I am alone but never a loner

I do not hear the laughter
Risky jokes among friends
I could not tell you if there's music
Or other noises to hear
I remember to smile
Act like I am involved
That I am listening
And laughing
For I have perfected this skill
But I am inside in my head
Dangerous thought running wild
Black upon blackness
Voices that aren't mine
I try my best to push them aside
To create room to pretend
But I am not present
For I am locked away
For today
tomorrow
All of eternity
I cannot escape
And I cannot tell
But I wish I hadn't perfected this facade

I yearn for a small crack to open
Just a small smidge of truth
So they could see what's truly inside me
A short escape of my darkness
I could share with my world
I would not have to speak of it for they would
'just know'
About this burden weighing heavy
Which would maybe become lighter
Or maybe become more
Once they realise the darkness
is just too dark to comprehend
They do not know how to fix me
Awkwardness shows it's face
They do not know what to say
To this soul they once knew
Maybe too far gone to come back
So forever I'll be this masked human
Closing those small cracks
So no more darkness falls through
Staying mine and mine only
Hiding perfectly inside
These shadows mine alone

For I am alone but never a loner

The Haiku

The season of change
Trees shed their exterior
As I do as well

A Question Existing

I no longer know who I am anymore. Where did
I go? Who is this girl looking back at me? I
don't recognise her face, her old soul, her tired
eyes? Who am I?…..

Am I the nurturing mother, strong and mild?
Or the dutiful daughter, gentle but wild?
A sister, a lover, a web tightly spun,
Do these roles define who I've become?

An employee, a cook, a housekeeper in stride,
A referee, a teacher, with love as my guide.
Each title vested, a weight on my soul,
Can one person truly embody them all?

A question,
A thought
A second too short
And I find myself again…..
A moment,
A glimpse of me

A crash
A cry, small voices who need me
And quickly back to the unrecognisable,

Again,
As I quickly put on a facade of indifference
Accepting that for the time being, I
Am
All
And every one of those things except me.

"Just forget about it"

He calls to me now and then you see
When I'm happy or at my peak
I hear his whispering voice with plea
Urging me, making me weak

Try as I might to resist his sweet song
He brings me back to a past
Filled with adventurous days so long
Those days always went by so fast

I forget my life now and do as he says
I'd do anything to go back right now
When I was entranced by your gaze,
When you swore you would love me by vow

But I was young, mindless, reckless, naive
What did I really know about love?
And when you went and took leave
You left me begging, praying up to above

Now I am grown you'd think I'd know better
But you show up now and again
Making me feel like I matter
But this isn't real love, it will not sustain

Do you remember your last fleeing words to me?
"Just forget about it" you said it so sharply
Those 4 words were said to set me free
But those 4 words tore my soul up so harshly

Your love for me it wasn't the real deal
I suffered for years upon end
I paid the price, paid the bill
Just heartbreak remains no one can mend

The unrequited

I'm right where you left me,
In this solitary realm I reside,
The world moves past, oblivious,
But my gaze remains deep inside.

Seasons change, their beauty unfolds,
Yet I'm blind to nature's tender cries,
Friends grow older, time slips away,
But my heart lingers where love lies.

In the stillness where you bid farewell,
Time halted, frozen in its embrace,
Since then, I haven't breathed right,
Lost in this lingering empty space.

I'm still right where you left me,
Recalling every moment captured and true,
Etched in the depths of my memory,
A tapestry of emotions, painted with you.

If only I knew on that fateful day,
That your presence would never depart,
I'd have walked past, untouched by fate,
Guarding my vulnerable, fragile heart.

But now I'm haunted by your face,
My dreams plagued by your tender smile,
And passing your house, memories ignite,
Resurrecting our love, even for a while.

Seventeen, lost in a fabricated fantasy,
Holding tight to moments so surreal,
Aching for a love that once consumed,
I'm still right where you left me to heal.

In nights of excess, when spirits run wild,
I stare at your number, my fingers tremble,
Yet my fearful mind refrains from the call,
Contemplating the words I'd assemble.

Would you answer, if I dared to speak?
Can you recall our moments, so pure,
Or have they faded in your realm of time,
Locked away, distant and obscure?

Under moonlit skies, we'd meet,
By the sea, love's symphony would play,
In shaded parks, beneath ancient trees,
Our souls entwined, lost in love's ballet.

Sneaking you into my home at twilight,
Only for my mother to catch your sight,
Glimmers of those stolen moments,
Etched in my mind, forever bright.

Accustomed to brokenness, never quite healed,
Yet I've learned to embrace the pain,
It's etched within my very being,
Those moments with you, an everlasting gain.

Oh, I wish I could forget,
Release these fragments of you,
But they persist, unwavering,
Every cherished moment, crystal clear and true.

I'm right where you left me,
In the depths of longing and rue,
For in each tender memory, a part of me held,
Never fading, forever marked, with a love so
true.

The sea lover

How do I always find myself here
When things don't always seem so clear
I go for a wander, just to clear my rough head
For lately my heart has been filled up with dread

An icy exterior, a mystery deep below
My breathing kind of softens, as your waves
flow
Your sharp crashing sounds
Beats in time as my heart pounds

Looking into your deep baby blues
My soul automatically relaxes on queue
My head seems a mess
Life's been a struggle, I silently confess

Breathe in and breathe out
Salty eyes theres no drought
As I walk beneath the moonlight
The Earth seems to still just for me tonight

Alas I'm much clearer
For I am right near her
Lapping gently at my feet in the night
Feeling stronger in myself it's time to take flight

Farewell until tomorrow, when I'll be back here
When again my head needs help to clear
For you are the only thing helping me mend
At least we'll be together at the sweet bitter end

The mental load

Endless lists, emails galore,
Appointments and homework, can't take
anymore.
School plays, Christmas do's, all on my plate,
Oh, and the cake stall? Well, add that to the
slate.

But wait, there's more, oh yes, don't you see?
I also have a job, taking care of more people,
what glee
Tasks upon tasks, the deadlines loom,
I sprint like a cheetah, zoom, zoom, zoom.

"Mum, can I have a biscuit?" you bellow from
the kitchen
But your dad was right there, I wish he'd pitch
in.
And in the chaos, my mind starts to brew,
Should I fetch it for you or send your dad's
rescue?

Dishes need cleaning, clothes need a wash,
Beds need changing, the floor needs a slosh.
What shall I cook for dinner tonight?
Oh, no! I forgot to defrost the meat, what a
fright.

Takeaway it is, our bellies are saved,
But the dog looks at me, feeling betrayed.
"We've run out of dog food!" I hear a voice
shout,
Off to the shop I go, no time to pout.

£100 spent, how did that occur?
Back home, the mess is absurd, I concur.
You ask, "What can I do?" expecting a list,
But my brain's overloaded, enough to persist.

I'll just do it myself, all on my own,
For I know it'll get done, with a monotone tone.
Asking for help? Oh, it's a hit or a miss,
When you're the default parent, it's unavoidable
bliss.

How do I care for myself in this never-ending
race?
Buried under piles, my own needs misplaced.
But let's find a solution, a moment to rest,
To rejuvenate, recharge, with a bit of zest.

For even in chaos, we must find our way,
To prioritize self-care, come what may.
The piles will shrink, the rest will align,
And I'll take a breather, just for a little time.

Binary stars

Two binary stars, their fate intertwined,
Bound by gravity's force, forever aligned.

Appearing as one, yet diverse in their form,
Unique exteriors, components that transform.

Given the choice, would they remain entwined,
Or seek to break free, their destinies redefined?

In a different realm, would they find delight,
An exhilarating existence, a celestial flight?

Or would they yearn, longing for their twin's
embrace,
Reuniting, forever bound in cosmic grace?

Ah, the allure of starting anew shines bright,
Yet pause for a moment, consider your current
light.

For what you possess, a connection so pure,
A bond that endures, unwavering and sure.

In seeking change blindly, tread with care,
Acknowledge the beauty that lies in your shared
air.

January and Mondays are the same

January's frost paints the world in white,
A hushed serenity, a tranquil sight.
Mondays, like thresholds, beckon us to begin,
To shed the past and let new chapters in.

Oh, January and Mondays, bound together so,
An intricate dance of progress and woe.
But in this month's chill and Mondays' strive,
Lies the chance for growth, to truly thrive.

So let January guide us, as Mondays persist,
To seize opportunities, to persistently resist,
The notion of stagnation, the fear of delay,
As we navigate January's and Mondays' sway.

Moving on

Does the sun miss the darkness, a realm
unknown,
Or does it revel in the brilliance it has always
shown?

Does the moon yearn for light, distant and
bright,
Or does it embrace patience, awaiting its
celestial delight?

Do trees long for their leaves when summer's
reign is through,
Or do they find joy in renewal, in starting anew?

Do flowers lament frost's touch, a trial they
endure,
Or do they hold faith in brighter days, their spirit
pure?

Do animals grieve when young ones venture to
roam,
Or do they celebrate freedom, finding solace in
their own?

Does the sea yearn for serenity, calm and serene,
Or does it dance with the tides, a majestic scene?

When loved ones depart, and sorrow tugs at our
soul,
Their essence lives on, forever intertwining,
making us whole.

You are not alone in longing, through every
passing year,
Yet, you have the power to let go, to embrace
what's near.

You, a part of nature's grand design, are bound
by its ways,
Feelings and emotions, a testament to the beauty
life portrays.

Will you feel this way forever, you may wonder
in despair,
But know, it's a journey, evolving with each
breath you bear.

Secrets lie not in permanence but in acceptance
and grace,
Embrace your feelings, for they're a part of the
human race.

You can find peace, dear soul, in knowing you're
not alone,
By accepting the dance of life, the ebb, and flow
it's shown.

The book poem

In lands afar, where dreams unfold,
I'll wander to the elves, so wise and old.
Or in the realm where wizards reside,
I'll seek enchantments, my soul to guide.

A throne awaits, fit for a queen,
A regal crown in a realm unseen.
To rule with grace, a kingdom to rise,
With majesty gleaming in vibrant skies.

Amidst friends, I'll feast and laugh with glee,
A symphony of joy, in harmony we'll be.
A table adorned with love and mirth,
A tapestry woven with camaraderie's worth.

A tiny tear that brims with sorrow's hue,
Or laughter's chorus that lifts the world anew.
In gentle moments, emotions may sway,
For in their dance, our spirits find their way.

Upon salty shores, the sea's scent I'll inhale,
Or the aroma of fresh bread, a tale to regale.
Freshly cut flowers, their fragrant allure,
Nature's bouquet, a gift so pure.

Feel the wind caress my flowing hair,
Or hailstones pricking the air with care.
Leaves beneath my feet, nature's golden rug,
Sensations whispered upon life's rugged path.

I'll turn the pages with eager delight,
Unveiling the story, with each word I ignite.
From chapter to chapter, a journey untold,
In realms of fantasy, my spirit takes hold.

Release me from the chains of mundane strife,
Let me drift on the currents of daydreams' life.
A respite from reality's sober demand,
Where imagination's embrace, forever I'll stand.

So take me, my books, where wonder can mend,
A poetic haven where souls ascend.
Let not my longing keep me confined,
In dreams, in words, true freedom I find.

Summers gone by

22

As the last of the summers suns warmth
Leaves the horizon,
My body shivers at thoughts.
For it knows what is coming,
On those long winter nights,
Where no colours or heat warm my numbing

Monday

Monday arrives like a child with sticky hands
Unwanted, unpleasant
But doesn't go away
Usually wet, grey and cold
Mimicking my feelings without meaning
We mask our indifference
Ready to face the outside world
But our feelings are still inside us
Though our outsides show different
Are we looking at smiling faces
But who feel like Monday inside
Maybe Mondays look like Mondays
But maybe truly feel like a Friday
If we can mask and be two things
Then maybe they mask as well
Who's to say that Mondays are Mondays
And that we all feel ok

Trust trauma

24

For you could only have known heartbreak
If you have already felt true love
Feelings that dance around each other
Trying not to touch
Never felt together
Life altering when you've felt either
But so easy to feel neither
When you haven't conquered the ability to trust

Karma

It is what it is, their choice to depart,
With no regard for the feelings in your heart.
They treat you like dirt, a shooting star shining
bright,
But fret not, my dear, let them go into the night.

Let them cheat, choose someone less worthy of
your grace,
But don't let them redefine your worth and erase.
Hold on to kindness, your strength, and your
power,
For your soul is radiant, even in the darkest hour.

Don't fall for their gaslighting, their narcissistic
games,
Their lies and manipulation, shifting blames.
You're worth more than they'll ever comprehend,
Their behavior, a reflection of the darkness they
tend.

No need to help them change, for karma will
take its turn,
The universe has a way, a lesson for them to
learn.

How they behave, it's not a reflection on your
being,
It speaks volumes about the flaws they're not
seeing.

If greatness eludes their eyes, blind to what's
right,
Then they don't deserve to witness your glorious
light.
Loyalty, a virtue they fail to uphold,
So let them go, your loyalty, untold.

You deserve better, a love that's true,
Someone who sees and appreciates all that is
you.
Let them leave, let them fade out of view,
For brighter horizons await, where love is
genuine and true.

Illusionist culture

27

To be truly you in a world filled with adversity,
betrayal and illusions
Is in itself a power and a strength that not many
possess for an entire existence

Although illusionists would disagree,
For that is their job to shrink your soul
To make you feel weak, less worthy
To take a piece you can't get back

Once you lie about your true self
It's impossible to get yourself back
For you will become a new illusionist
And on and on the cult grows

A mothers love

From the moment that plus sign appeared,
Life transformed, my heart overwhelmed, I
feared.
My mind, a constant worry, always in a whirl,
Oh, the joys and uncertainties of being a mother,
my precious pearl.

For as a mother, we find ourselves at the back,
Putting your needs before ours, our own desires
off track.
Our freedom surrender, for your well-being we
strive,
With every sacrifice, the greatest love we derive.

Ten tiny fingers, ten tiny toes,
Oh, the miracle of my body, oh how you grow.
To nourish and protect you, my dear,
A marvel of creation, pure and sincere.

Love, oh love, an emotion beyond compare,
Like sunbeams filling my heart, so rare.
Never before have I felt such pure bliss,
Every moment with you, a heavenly kiss.

As you blossom, walking and talking with grace,

I watch in awe, love shining on my face.
Then comes the day you venture to nursery and
beyond,
But worry not, my love, for my thoughts will
correspond.

I long for you all day, can't wait to reunite,
To cradle you in my arms and hold you so tight.
Immersed in your sweet scent, we find solace in
each other,
Home, where your presence brings warmth like
no other.

As you grow older, my grip must loosen, I know,
But in my heart, you'll forever be my sweet
baby, a love that will not go.
In every step you take, every milestone you
achieve,
I'll be beside you, even when you leave.

For the bond between mother and child is
eternal,
A love that transcends time, so pure, so internal.
So grow, my dear, explore and soar,
Know that my love for you will endure
evermore.

Lose it all

It's a miscarriage of justice
Losing you this way
Everything was fine
You were going to be mine

My soul broke in two
And the earth ceased to spin
The air stilled at once
On that grey September month

It's not just you that had gone
It's all of my dreams and hopes too
I've lost nights without sleep
Tears that you'd weep

I will never be the same again
Though they expect that I will be fine
Forget what has happened
Ashes have been blackened

This emptiness inside swallows me up
I'll miss you forever and a day
The griefs always there
Some days I can't bare

I envision who you'd be,
Who's hair, who's nose or smile
Never got to say your name
Am I to blame?

I'll miss you for forever and a day
Until we meet again
When heaven opens up for me
I cannot wait for that day to see

Oh how the sun will shine
When again you are mine
You'll be so glad I came
When I can finally call your name

Finding Happiness

Everyone searches for happiness,
In the depths of desires and material things,
But have we forsaken the simpler joys,
The beauty that nature so gracefully brings?

Listen closely to the gentle chirps,
The melodies of birds perched on high,
Their songs a reminder of pure bliss,
A symphony that stirs the heart and sky.

Feel the buzz of the humble bees,
As they dance amidst flowers so fair,
Their delicate wings a mesmerizing hum,
A reminder to appreciate life's sweet air.

Let the wind whisper through your hair,
Caressing your spirit, setting it free,
In its gentle caress, find solace and peace,
A reminder of life's profound harmony.

Embrace the spray of the mighty sea,
Its briny touch upon your skin,
Let the waves sing their timeless tune,
A reminder of the infinite depths within.

For happiness lies not in material gain,
Nor solely in the embrace of others we seek,
But in the beauty of everyday moments,
In nature's treasures, so tender and meek.

So let us not forget the simpler joys,
The chirps, the buzz, the wind, the sea,
For true happiness is found in gratitude,
In the profound beauty of life's simplicity.

The end

The end looms near, yet fear eludes me,
Passing through this realm, my soul set free.
My turn to depart, to explore the unknown,
Seeking different worlds, dreams yet unblown.

Reunion awaits with those cherished and lost,
Embracing anew, counting the moments, the
cost.
Conversations held in the spaces between,
Where pain and sadness dissolve into serene.

Leaving this world for others to embrace,
Delighting in passing on, a change of pace.
Let me impart advice, an earnest plea,
Choose kindness, even when kindness runs free.

Stand strong in beliefs, resist persuasion's pull,
Embrace loved ones, laughter's gentle lull.
Persistence fuels success, idleness stalls,
Treasure the wind's touch, fragrant grass, ocean's
calls.

Take respite, unwind, seek solace and peace,
Lend a helping hand, let karma find release.
When your time comes, as mine inevitably will,

Greet it like an old friend, every moment
fulfilled.
35

For a life unrestrained, free from remorse,
No regrets defined, no limits in its course.